ELEVEN MYTHS ABOUT

THE TUSKEGEE AIRMEN

ALSO BY DAN HAULMAN

*The United States Air Force and
Humanitarian Airlift Operations, 1947–1994* (1998)

*Air Force Aerial Victory Credits:
World War I, World War II, Korea, and Vietnam* (1988)

*One Hundred Years of Flight: USAF Chronology of
Significant Air and Space Events, 1903–2002* (2003)

Inspirations (2005)

The Tuskegee Airmen: An Illustrated History (2011)

*The Tuskegee Airmen and the
"Never Lost a Bomber" Myth* (2011)

*What Hollywood Got Right and Wrong about the Tuskegee Airmen
in the Great New Movie, Red Tails* (2012)

ELEVEN MYTHS
ABOUT THE
TUSKEGEE
AIRMEN

DANIEL HAULMAN

NEWSOUTH BOOKS

Montgomery

NewSouth Books
105 S. Court Street
Montgomery, AL 36104

Library of Congress Cataloging-in-Publication Data

Haulman, Daniel L. (Daniel Lee), 1949-
Eleven myths about the Tuskegee Airmen / Dan Haulman.

p. cm.

Includes bibliographical references and index.

ISBN 978-1-60306-147-6 (pbk.) -- ISBN 1-60306-147-9 (pbk.)
ISBN 978-1-60306-148-3 (ebook) -- ISBN 1-60306-148-7 (ebook)

1. United States. Army Air Forces. Fighter Group, 332nd--History. 2. World
War, 1939-1945--Participation, African American. 3. World War, 1939-1945--
Aerial operations, American. 4. African American air pilots--History. 5. United
States. Army Air Forces. Air Force, 15th--History. [1. Tuskegee Army Air Field
(Ala.)--History.] I. Title.
D790.252332nd .H38 2012
940.54'4973--dc23

2011052274

Printed in the United States of America

I would like to dedicate this
to the late Lt. Col. William H. Holloman III,
one of the original Tuskegee Airmen. I knew him well.

Contents

Introduction

The members of the 332d Fighter Group and the 99th, 100th, 301st, and 302d Fighter Squadrons during World War II are remembered in part because they were the only African-American pilots who served in combat with the Army Air Forces during World War II. Because they trained at Tuskegee Army Air Field before and during the war, they are sometimes called the Tuskegee Airmen. In the more than sixty years since World War II, several stories have grown up about the Tuskegee Airmen, some of them true and some of them false. This paper focuses on eleven myths about the Tuskegee Airmen that, in light of the historical documentation available at the Air Force Historical Research Agency, and sources at the Air University Library, are not accurate. That documentation includes monthly histories of the 99th Fighter Squadron, the 332d Fighter Group and the 477th Bombardment Group, the 332d Fighter Group's daily narrative mission reports, orders issued by the Twelfth and Fifteenth Air Forces, Fifteenth Air Force mission folders, and missing air crew reports.

I will address each of the following eleven myths separately:

1. The Myth of Inferiority
2. The Myth of "Never Lost a Bomber"
3. The Myth of the Deprived Ace
4. The Myth of Being First to Shoot Down German Jets
5. The Myth that the Tuskegee Airmen sank a German destroyer
6. The Myth of the "Great Train Robbery"
7. The Myth of Superiority
8. The Myth that the Tuskegee Airmen units were all black
9. The Myth that all Tuskegee Airmen were fighter pilots who flew red-

ELEVEN MYTHS ABOUT THE TUSKEGEE AIRMEN

Myth 1

Inferiority

T he first misconception regarding the Tuskegee Airmen was that they were inferior. The myth was that black pilots could not perform as well in combat as their white counterparts. This misconception developed even before the 99th Fighter Squadron deployed as the first African-American Army Air Forces organization in combat. On October 30, 1925, the War College of the U.S. Army issued a memorandum entitled, "The Use of Negro Manpower in War." The memorandum noted that Negroes were inferior to whites and encouraged continued segregation within the Army.[1] Even during the squadron's operations in North Africa, authorities challenged its right to remain in combat.

In September 1943, Major General Edwin J. House, commander of the XII Air Support Command, sent a memorandum to Maj. Gen. John K. Cannon, Deputy Commander of the Northwest African Tactical Air Force, suggesting that the 99th Fighter Squadron had failed to demonstrate effectiveness in combat, and should be taken out of the combat zone. The memorandum was based on information from Col. William Momyer, commander of the 33rd Fighter Group, to which the 99th Fighter Squadron had been attached.[2]

Following the House memorandum, which went up the chain of command all the way to the headquarters of the Army Air Forces, the Statistical Control Division, Office of Management Control, War Department, conducted an official study to compare the performance of the 99th Fighter Squadron with that of other P-40 units in the Twelfth Air Force. The subsequent report, released on March 30, 1944, concluded that the 99th Fighter Squadron had performed as well as the other squadrons.[3]

As you can see from the table below, there were seven fighter groups of the Fifteenth Air Force flying primarily bomber escort missions between

June 1944 and the end of April 1945. In terms of aerial victory credits, which is one good measure of combat performance, the 332d Fighter Group did not score the lowest number. In fact, its total number of aerial victory credits was higher than that of two of the white groups.

Table I: Fighter Groups of the Fifteenth Air Force in World War II

Organization	Aerial victories June 1944–April 1945
1st Fighter Group	72
14th Fighter Group	85
31st Fighter Group	278
52d Fighter Group	224.5
82d Fighter Group	106
325th Fighter Group	252
332d Fighter Group	94

Sources: USAF Historical Study No. 85, "USAF Credits for the Destruction of Enemy Aircraft, World War II" (Washington, DC: Office of Air Force History, 1978); Maurer Maurer, *Air Force Combat Units of World War II* (Washington, DC: Office of Air Force History, 1983).

I should mention, however, that both of the groups scoring lower numbers of aerial victories than the Tuskegee Airmen in the same period were flying P-38 aircraft, and the 332d Fighter Group was flying, for all but one month of the period, P-51 aircraft, which had a higher speed and range than the P-38s. Of the four P-51 fighter groups in the Fifteenth Air Force, the 31st, 52nd, 325th, and 332nd, the 332nd Fighter Group shot down fewer enemy aircraft in the same period. It is possible that the Tuskegee Airmen shot down fewer enemy aircraft than the other P-51 fighter groups, and did not have any aces, because they were staying closer to the bombers they were escorting, as ordered, and not abandoning the bombers to chase after enemy aircraft in the distance. Twenty-seven of the bombers in groups the 332d Fighter Group was assigned to escort were shot down by enemy aircraft. The average number of bombers shot down by enemy aircraft while under the escort of the other groups of the Fifteenth Air Force was 46. The Tuskegee Airmen lost significantly fewer bombers than the average number lost by the other fighter groups in the Fifteenth Air Force.

Brigadier General Benjamin O. Davis Sr., the first African American general in the U.S. Army, awards the Distinguished Flying Cross to his son, Colonel Benjamin O. Davis, Jr., for a mission the younger Davis led on June 9, 1944.

Myth 2

"Never Lost a Bomber"

nother misconception that developed during the last months of the war is the story that no bomber under escort by the Tuskegee Airmen was ever shot down by enemy aircraft. A version of this misconception appears in Alan Gropman's book, *The Air Force Integrates* (Washington, DC: Office of Air Force History, 1985), p. 14: "Their record on escort duty remained unparalleled. They never lost an American bomber to enemy aircraft." This misconception originated even before the end of World War II, in the press. A version of the statement first appeared in a March 10, 1945 issue of *Liberty Magazine*, in an article by Roi Ottley, who claimed that the black pilots had not lost a bomber they escorted to enemy aircraft in more than 100 missions. The 332d Fighter Group had by then flown more than 200 missions. Two weeks after the Ottley article, on March 24, 1945, another article appeared in the *Chicago Defender*, claiming that in more than 200 missions, the group had not lost a bomber they escorted to enemy aircraft. In reality, bombers under Tuskegee Airmen escort were shot down on seven different days: June 9, 1944; June 13, 1944; July 12, 1944; July 18, 1944; July 20, 1944; August 24, 1944; and March 24, 1945.[4] Moreover, the Tuskegee Airmen flew 311 missions for the Fifteenth Air Force between early June 1944 and late April 1945, and only 179 of those missions escorted bombers.

Alan Gropman interviewed General Benjamin O. Davis, Jr., years after World War II, and specifically asked him if the "never lost a bomber" statement were true. General Davis replied that he questioned the statement, but that it had been repeated so many times people were coming to believe it (AFHRA call number K239.0512-1922).[5] Davis himself must have known the statement was not true, because his own citation for the Distinguished Flying Cross, contained in Fifteenth Air Force General Order 2972 dated August 31, 1944, noted that on June 9, 1944, "Colonel Davis so skillfully disposed his squadrons that in spite of the large number of enemy fighters, the bomber formation suffered only a few losses."[6]

In order to determine whether or not bombers under the escort of the Tuskegee Airmen were ever shot down by enemy aircraft during World War II, I practiced the following method.

First, I determined which bombardment wing the Tuskegee Airmen were escorting on a given day, and when and where that escort took place. I found this information in the daily narrative mission reports of the 332d Fighter Group, which are filed with the group's monthly histories from World War II. The call number for these documents at the Air Force Historical Research Agency is GP-332-HI followed by the month and year.

Next, I determined which bombardment groups were in the bombardment wing that the Tuskegee Airmen were escorting on the day in question. I found this information in the daily mission folders of the Fifteenth Air Force. The Fifteenth Air Force daily mission folders also contain narrative mission reports for all the groups that took part in missions on any given day, including reports of both the fighter and bombardment groups, as well as the wings to which they belonged. The call number for these documents at the Air Force Historical Research Agency is 670.332 followed by the date. The bombardment group daily mission reports show which days bombers of the group were shot down by enemy aircraft.

Next, I checked the index of the Missing Air Crew Reports, to see if the groups that the Tuskegee Airmen were escorting that day lost any aircraft. If any aircraft of those groups were lost that day, I recorded the missing air crew report numbers. This index of Missing Air Crew Reports is located in the archives branch of the Air Force Historical Research Agency. The Missing Air Crew Reports usually confirmed the bomber loss information contained in the bombardment group daily narrative mission reports.

Finally, I looked at the individual Missing Air Crew Reports of the Tuskegee Airmen-escorted groups that lost airplanes on that day to see when the airplanes were lost, where the airplanes were lost, and whether the airplanes were lost because of enemy aircraft fire, enemy antiaircraft fire, or some other cause. The Missing Air Crew Reports note that information for each aircraft lost, with the aircraft type and serial number, and usually also contain witness statements that describe the loss. For lost bombers, the witnesses were usually the crew members of other bombers in the same formation, or members of the crews of the lost bombers themselves, after they returned. The Missing Air Crew Reports are filed on microfiche in the archives branch of the Air Force Historical Research Agency.

Using this procedure, I determined conclusively that on at least seven days, bombers under the escort of the Tuskegee Airmen's 332d Fighter Group were shot down by enemy aircraft. Those days include June 9, 1944; June 13, 1944; July 12, 1944; July 18, 1944; July 20, 1944; August 24, 1944; and March 24, 1945.[7]

Table II: Bombers Shot Down by Enemy Aircraft while Flying in Groups the 332D Fighter Group was Assigned to Escort

Date	Time	Location	Type	Serial Number	WG	Group	Missing Air Crew Report
9 June 1944	0905	46 40 N, 12 40 E	B-24	42-78219	304	459	6317
9 June 1944	0907	46 00 N, 12 40 E	B-24	42-52318	304	459	6179
13 June 1944	0900	Porogruardo, Italy	B-24	42-94741	49	484	6097
12 July 1944	1050	20 miles SE of Mirabeau, France	B-24	42-52723	49	461	6894
12 July 1944	1051	10 miles E of Mirabeau, France	B-24	42-78202	49	461	6895
12 July 1944	1105	43 43 N, 05 23 E	B-24	42-78291	49	461	7034
18 July 1944	1045–1100	near Memmingen	B-17	42-107179	5	483	6856
18 July 1944	1045–1100	near Memmingen	B-17	42-107008	5	483	6953
18 July 1944	1045–1100	near Memmingen	B-17	42-102862	5	483	6954
18 July 1944	1045–1100	near Memmingen	B-17	44-6174	5	483	6975
18 July 1944	1045–1100	near Memmingen	B-17	42-97671	5	483	6976

18 July 1944	1045–1100	near Memmingen	B-17	42-102382	5	483	6977
18 July 1944	1045–1100	near Memmingen	B-17	42-107170	5	483	6978
18 July 1944	1045–1100	near Memmingen	B-17	42-102923	5	483	6979
18 July 1944	1045–1100	near Memmingen	B-17	42-102927	5	483	6980
18 July 1944	1045–1100	near Memmingen	B-17	42-97584	5	483	6981
18 July 1944	1045–1100	near Memmingen	B-17	42-46267	5	483	7097
18 July 1944	1045–1100	near Memmingen	B-17	42-102422	5	483	7098
18 July 1944	1045–1100	near Memmingen	B-17	44-6177	5	483	7099
18 July 1944	1045–1100	near Memmingen	B-17	42-107172	5	483	7153
18 July 1944	1104	47 54 N, 10 40 E	B-17	42-102943	5	301	7310
20 Jul 1944	1000	45 38 N, 12 28 E	B-24	44-40886	55	485	6914
20 Jul 1944	0954	45 38 N, 12 28 E	B-24	42-78361	55	485	6919
24 Aug 1944	1245–1247	49 28 N, 15 25 E	B-17	42-31645	5	97	7971
24 Mar 1945	1200	52 05 N, 13 10 E	B-17	44-6283	5	463	13278
24 Mar 1945	1208	51 00 N, 13 10 E	B-17	44-6761	5	463	13274
24 Mar 1945	1227	Berlin target area	B-17	44-8159	5	463	13375

Primary Sources: Daily mission reports of the 332d Fighter Group (Air Force Historical Research Agency call number GP-332-HI); Daily mission reports of the bombardment groups the 332d Fighter Group was assigned to escort per day, from the daily mission folders of the Fifteenth Air Force (Air Force Historical Research Agency call number 670.332); Microfiche of Missing Air Crew Reports (MACRs) at the Air Force Historical Research Agency, indexed by date and group.

The *Chicago Defender* article of March 24, 1945 that helped create the "never lost a bomber myth."

Myth 3

The Deprived Ace

Another popular story that circulated after World War II which is not true is that white officers were determined to prevent any black man in the Army Air Forces from becoming an ace, and therefore reduced the aerial victory credit total of Lee Archer from five to less than five to accomplish their aim. A version of this misconception appears in the Oliver North compilation, *War Stories III* ((Washington, DC: Regnery Publishing, Inc., 2005), p. 152.[8] In reality, according to the World War II records of the 332d Fighter Group and its squadrons, which were very carefully kept by members of the group, Lee Archer claimed a total of four aerial victories during World War II, and received credit for every claim.[9]

The myth that Lee Archer was an ace was perpetuated in part because of an excerpt in the book *The Tuskegee Airmen* (Boston: Bruce Humphries, Inc., 1955), by Charles E. Francis. In that book, Francis notes an aerial victory for July 20, 1944, but the history of the 332d Fighter Group for July 1944, the mission report of the 332d Fighter Group for July 20, 1944, and the aerial victory credit orders issued by the Fifteenth Air Force in 1944 do not support the claim.[10]

World War II documents, including monthly histories of the 332d Fighter Group and Twelfth and Fifteenth Air Force general orders awarding aerial victory credits show that Lee Archer claimed and was awarded a total of four aerial victory credits during World War II, one on July 18, 1944, and three on October 12, 1944. There is no evidence among these documents that Lee Archer ever claimed any more than four enemy aircraft destroyed in the air during the war, and he was never awarded any more than four. A fifth was never taken away or downgraded to half. Moreover, there is no evidence, among the documents, that there was any effort to prevent any members of the 332d Fighter Group from becoming an ace. When claims were made, they were recorded and evaluated by a victory credit board that decided, using witness statements and gun camera film, whether to award credits, which were confirmed by general orders of the Fifteenth Air Force. There is no evidence that the black claims were treated any differently than the white claims. If there had been such discrimination in the evaluation of claims, Colonel Benjamin O. Davis, Jr., the leader of the group would have most likely complained, and there is no evidence of any such complaint. To think that someone or some group was totaling the number of aerial victory credits of each of the members of the various squadrons of the 332d Fighter Group and intervening to deny credit to anyone who might become an ace is not consistent with the aerial victory credit procedures of the day.

Table III: Chronological Table of 332d Fighter Group Aerial Victory Credits

Date	Name	Unit	Downed	GO #
2 Jul 1943	1 Lt Charles B. Hall	99 FS	1 FW-190	32 XII ASC 7 Sep 43
27 Jan 1944	2 Lt Clarence W. Allen	99 FS	0.5 FW-190	66 XII AF 24 May 44
	1 Lt Willie Ashley Jr.	99 FS	1 FW-190	122 XII AF 7 Aug 44
	2 Lt Charles P. Bailey	99 FS	1 FW-190	66 XII AF 24 May 44
	1 Lt Howard Baugh	99 FS	1 FW-190	122 XII AF 7 Aug 44
			0.5 FW-190	66 XII AF 24 May 44
	Cpt Lemuel R. Custis	99 FS	1 FW-190	122 XII AF 7 Aug 44
	1 Lt Robert W. Deiz	99 FS	1 FW-190	66 XII AF 24 May 44
	2 Lt Wilson V. Eagleson	99 FS	1 FW-190	66 XII AF 24 May 44
	1 Lt Leon C. Roberts	99 FS	1 FW-190	122 XII AF 7 Aug 44
	2 Lt Lewis C. Smith	99 FS	1 FW-190	66 XII AF 24 May 44
	1 Lt Edward L. Toppins	99 FS	1 FW-190	81 XII AF 22 Jun 44
28 Jan 1944	1 Lt Robert W. Deiz	99 FS	1 FW-190	122 XII AF 7 Aug 44
	Cpt Charles B. Hall		1 FW-190	64 XII AF 22 May 44
			1 ME-109	
5 Feb 1944	1 Lt Elwood T. Driver	99 FS	1 FW-190	66 XII AF 24 May 44

Date	Name	Squadron	Enemy Aircraft	Mission
7 Feb 1944	2 Lt Wilson V. Eagleson	99 FS	1 FW-190	122 XII AF 7 Aug 44
	2 Lt Leonard M. Jackson	99 FS	1 FW-190	66 XII AF 24 May 44
	1 Lt Clinton B. Mills	99 FS	1 FW-190	66 XII AF 24 May 44
9 Jun 1944	1 Lt Charles M. Bussy	302 FS	1 ME-109	1473 XV AF 30 Jun 44
	2 Lt Frederick D. Funderburg	301 FS	2 ME-109s	1473 XV AF 30 Jun 44
	1 Lt Melvin T. Jackson	302 FS	1 ME-109	1473 XV AF 30 Jun 44
	1 Lt Wendell O. Pruitt	302 FS	1 ME-109	1473 XV AF 30 Jun 44
12 Jul 1944	1 Lt Harold E. Sawyer	301 FS	1 FW-190	2032 XV AF 23 Jul 44
	1 Lt Joseph D. Elsberry	301 FS	3 FW-190	2466 XV AF Aug 44
16 Jul 1944	1 Lt Alfonza W. Davis	332 FG	1 MA-205	2030 XV AF 23 Jul 44
	2 Lt William W. Green Jr	302 FS	1 MA-202	2029 XV AF 23 Jul 44
17 Jul 1944	1 Lt Luther H. Smith Jr.	302 FS	1 ME-109	2350 XV AF 6 Aug 44
	2 Lt Robert H. Smith	302 FS	1 ME-109	2350 XV AF 6 Aug 44
	1 Lt Laurence D. Wilkins	302 FS	1 ME-109	2350 XV AF 6 Aug 44
18 Jul 1944	2 Lt Lee A. Archer	302 FS	1 ME-109	2350 XV AF 6 Aug 44
	1 Lt Charles P. Bailey	99 FS	1 FW-190	2484 XV AF 11 Aug 44
	1 Lt Weldon K. Groves	302 FS	1 ME-109	2350 XV AF 6 Aug 44
18 Jul 1944	1 Lt Jack D. Holsclaw	100 FS	2 ME-109s	2202 XV AF 31 Jul 44
	2 Lt Clarence D. Lester	100 FS	3 ME-109s	2202 XV AF 31 Jul 44

Date	Name	Squadron	Claim	Citation
18 Jul 1944	2 Lt Walter J. A. Palmer	100 FS	1 ME-109	2202 XV AF 31 Jul 44
	2 Lt Roger Romine	302 FS	1 ME-109	2350 XV AF 6 Aug 44
	Cpt Edward L. Toppins	99 FS	1 FW-190	2484 XV AF 11 Aug 44*
	2 Lt Hugh S. Warner	302 FS	1 ME-109	2350 XV AF 6 Aug 44
20 Jul 1944	Cpt Joseph D. Elsberry	301 FS	1 ME-109	2284 XV AF 3 Aug 44
	1 Lt Langdon E. Johnson	100 FS	1 ME-109	2202 XV AF 31 Jul 44
	Cpt Armour G. McDaniel	301 FS	1 ME-109	2284 XV AF 3 Aug 44
	Cpt Edward L. Toppins	99 FS	1 ME-109	2484 XV AF 11 Aug 44
25 Jul 1944	1 Lt Harold E. Sawyer	301 FS	1 ME-109	2284 XV AF 3 Aug 44
26 Jul 1944	1 Lt Freddie E. Hutchins	302 FS	1 ME-109	2350 XV AF 6 Aug 44
	1 Lt Leonard M. Jackson	99 FS	1 ME-109	2484 XV AF 11 Aug 44
	2 Lt Roger Romine	302 FS	1 ME-109	2350 XV AF 6 Aug 44
	Cpt Edward L. Toppins	99 FS	1 ME-109	2484 XV AF 11 Aug 44
27 Jul 1944	1 Lt Edward C. Gleed	301 FS	2 FW-190s	2284 XV AF 3 Aug 44
	2 Lt Alfred M. Gorham	301 FS	2 FW-190s	2284 XV AF 3 Aug 44
	Cpt Claude B. Govan	301 FS	1 ME-109	2284 XV AF 3 Aug 44
	2 Lt Richard W. Hall	100 FS	1 ME-109	2485 XV AF 11 Aug 44
	1 Lt Leonard M. Jackson	99 FS	1 ME-109	2484 XV AF 11 Aug 44
	1 Lt Felix J. Kirkpatrick	302 FS	1 ME-109	2350 XV AF 6 Aug 44

Date	Pilot	FS	Enemy Aircraft	Credit
30 Jul 1944	2 Lt Carl E. Johnson	100 FS	1 RE-2001	2485 XV AF 11 Aug 44
14 Aug 1944	2 Lt George M. Rhodes Jr.	100 FS	1 FW-190	2831 XV AF 25 Aug 44
23 Aug 1944	FO William L. Hill	302 FS	1 ME-109	3538 XV AF 21 Sep 44
24 Aug 1944	1 Lt John F. Briggs	100 FS	1 ME-109	3153 XV AF 6 Sep 44
	1 Lt Charles E. McGee	302 FS	1 FW-190	3174 XV AF 7 Sep 44
	1 Lt William H. Thomas	302 FS	1 FW-190	449 XV AF 31 Jan 45
12 Oct 1944	1 Lt Lee A. Archer	302 FS	3 ME-109s	4287 XV AF 1 Nov 44
	Cpt Milton R. Brooks	302 FS	1 ME-109	4287 XV AF 1 Nov 44
	1 Lt William W. Green Jr.	302 FS	1 HE-111	4287 XV AF 1 Nov 44
	Cpt Wendell O. Pruitt	302 FS	1 HE-111 / 1 ME-109	4287 XV AF 1 Nov 44
	1 Lt Roger Romine	302 FS	1 ME-109	4287 XV AF 1 Nov 44
	1 Lt Luther H. Smith Jr.	302 FS	1 HE-111	4604 XV AF 21 Nov 44
16 Nov 1944	Cpt Luke J. Weathers	302 FS	2 ME-109s	4990 XV AF 13 Dec 44
16 Mar 1945	1 Lt William S. Price III	301 FS	1 ME-109	1734 XV AF 24 Mar 45
24 Mar 1945	2 Lt Charles V. Brantley	100 FS	1 ME-262	2293 XV AF 12 Apr 45
	1 Lt Roscoe C. Brown	100 FS	1 ME-262	2293 XV AF 12 Apr 45
	1 Lt Earl R. Lane	100 FS	1 ME-262	2293 XV AF 12 Apr 45

Date	Name	FS	Claim	Record
31 Mar 1945	2 Lt Raul W. Bell	100 FS	1 FW-190	2293 XV AF 12 Apr 45
	2 Lt Thomas P. Brasswell	99 FS	1 FW-190	2292 XV AF 12 Apr 45
	1 Lt Roscoe C. Brown	100 FS	1 FW-190	2293 XV AF 12 Apr 45
	Maj William A. Campbell	99 FS	1 ME-109	2292 XV AF 12 Apr 45
	2 Lt John W. Davis	99 FS	1 ME-109	2292 XV AF 12 Apr 45
	2 Lt James L. Hall	99 FS	1 ME-109	2292 XV AF 12 Apr 45
31 Mar 1945	1 Lt Earl R. Lane	100 FS	1 ME-109	2293 XV AF 12 Apr 45
	FO John H. Lyle	100 FS	1 ME-109	2293 XV AF 12 Apr 45
	1 Lt Daniel L. Rich	99 FS	1 ME-109	2292 XV AF 12 Apr 45
	2 Lt Hugh J. White	99 FS	1 ME-109	2292 XV AF 12 Apr 45
	1 Lt Robert W. Williams	100 FS	2 FW-190s	2293 XV AF 12 Apr 45
	2 Lt Bertram W. Wilson Jr.	100 FS	1 FW-190	2293 XV AF 12 Apr 45
1 Apr 1945	2 Lt Carl E. Carey	301 FS	2 FW-190s	2294 XV AF 12 Apr 45
	2 Lt John E. Edwards	301 FS	2 ME-109s	2294 XV AF 12 Apr 45
	FO James H. Fischer	301 FS	1 FW-190	2294 XV AF 12 Apr 45
	2 Lt Walter P. Manning	301 FS	1 FW-190	2294 XV AF 12 Apr 45
	2 Lt Harold M. Morris	301 FS	1 FW-190	2294 XV AF 12 Apr 45
	1 Lt Harry T. Stewart	301 FS	3 FW-190s	2294 XV AF 12 Apr 45
	1 Lt Charles L. White	301 FS	2 ME-109s	2294 XV AF 12 Apr 45

15 Apr 1945	1 Lt Jimmy Lanham	301 FS	1 ME-109	3484 XV AF 29 May 45
26 Apr 1945	2 Lt Thomas W. Jefferson	301 FS	2 ME-109s	3362 XV AF 23 May 45
	1 Lt Jimmy Lanham	301 FS	1 ME-109	3362 XV AF 23 May 45
	2 Lt Richard A. Simons	100 FS	1 ME-109	2990 XV AF 4 May 45

*Order says credit was 16 Jul 1944, but history says 18 Jul 1944

During World War II, the only African-American pilots in the Army Air Forces who flew in combat served in the 99th, 100th, 301st, and 302nd Fighter Squadrons and the 332nd Fighter Group. None of these pilots earned more than four aerial victory credits. None of them became an ace, with at least five aerial victory credits. Were the Tuskegee Airmen who earned four aerial victory credits sent home in order to prevent a black pilot from becoming an ace?

That is very doubtful. First Lieutenant Lee Archer was deployed back to the United States the month after he scored his fourth aerial victory credit, and the same month he received his fourth aerial victory credit. Captain Edward Toppins was deployed back to the United States the second month after he scored his fourth aerial victory credit, and the month after he received credit for it. However, Captain Joseph Elsberry earned his fourth aerial victory credit in July 1944, and received credit for it early in August 1944. He did not redeploy to the United States until December 1944. If there was a policy of sending Tuskegee Airmen with four aerial victory credits home, in order to prevent a black man from becoming an ace, the case of Captain Joseph Elsberry contradicts it, because he was not sent home until four months after his fourth aerial victory credit was awarded, and five months after he scored it. It is more likely that the pilots who deployed back to the United States did so after having completed the number of missions they needed to finish their respective tours of duty.

Table IV: Table of Tuskegee Airmen with Four Aerial Victories

Name and rank at time of fourth aerial victory credit	Fighter Group	Fighter Squadron	Date of fourth aerial victory	Date of award of fourth aerial victory credit	Month of redeployment to the United States
1st Lt Lee Archer	332	302	12 October 1944	1 Nov 1944	November 1944
Captain Joseph Elsberry	332	301	20 July 1944	3 Aug 1944	December 1944
Captain Edward Toppins	332	99	26 July 1944	11 Aug 1944	September 1944

Sources: Fifteenth Air Force general orders awarding aerial victory credits; monthly histories of the 332d Fighter Group for August, September, October, November, and December 1944. Researcher: Daniel L. Haulman, Historian, Air Force Historical Research Agency

Myth 4

Being the First to Shoot Down German Jets

Sometimes one hears the claim that the Tuskegee Airmen were the first to shoot down German jets.[11] Three Tuskegee Airmen, 1st Lt. Roscoe Brown, 1st Lt. Earl R. Lane, and 2nd Lt. Charles V. Brantley, each shot down a German Me-262 jet on March 24, 1945, during the longest Fifteenth Air Force mission, which went all the way to Berlin.[12] However, American pilots shot down no less than sixty Me-262 aircraft before March 24, 1945. Most of these American pilots served in the Eighth Air Force.[13]

The Tuskegee Airmen were also not the first Fifteenth Air Force pilots to shoot down German jets, as is sometimes alledged.[14] Two such pilots, 1st Lt. Eugene P. McGlauflin and 2d Lt. Roy L. Scales, both of the Fifteenth Air Force's 31st Fighter Group and 308th Fighter Squadron, shared a victory over an Me-262 German jet on December 22, 1944, and Capt. William J. Dillard, also of the Fifteenth Air Force's 31st Fighter Group and 308th Fighter Squadron, shot down an Me-262 German jet on March 22, 1945.

Table V: Fifteenth Air Force Aerial Victories over German Me-262 Jets before March 24, 1945

Rank	Name	Organization	Date	Credits	Aircraft shot down	Authority
1 Lt.	Eugene P. McGlaufin	308th Fighter Sq, 31st Fighter Gp, Fifteenth AF	22 Dec 1944	0.5	Me-262	15 AF GO 327, issued 22 Jan 1945
2 Lt.	Roy L. Scales	308th Fighter Sq, 31st Fighter Gp, Fifteenth AF	22 Dec 1944	0.5	Me-262	15 AF GO 327, issued 22 Jan 1945
Capt	William J. Dillard	308th Fighter Sq, 31st Fighter Gp, Fifteenth AF	22 Mar 1945	1.00	Me-262	15 AF GO 2591, issued 21 Apr 1945

Sources: Fifteenth Air Force General Order 327 dated Jan 22, 1945, p. 2, under call number 670.193 at Air Force Historical Research Agency; Fifteenth Air Force General Order 2591 dated Apr. 21, 1945, p. 3, under call number 670.193 at Air Force Historical Research Agency; 308 Fighter Squadron History, Jan 1942-Jun 1945, under call number SQ-FI-308-HI at Air Force Historical Research Agency.

Moreover, on the day three Tuskegee Airmen shot down three German jets over Berlin on March 24, 1945, five other American pilots of the Fifteenth Air Force, on the same mission, with the 31st Fighter Group, also shot down German Me-262 jets. They included Colonel William A. Daniel, 1st Lt. Forrest M. Keene, 1st Lt Raymond D. Leonard, Capt. Kenneth T. Smith, and 2nd Lt. William M. Wilder.[15]

Myth 5

The Tuskegee Airmen Sank a German Destroyer

The 332d Fighter Group mission report for June 25, 1944 notes that the group sank a German destroyer in the Adriatic Sea near Trieste that day. The pilots on that mission undoubtedly believed they had sunk a German destroyer, but other records cast doubt on whether the ship actually sank.

The only German ship in the Trieste area of the Adriatic Sea reported to have been hit by Allied aircraft on June 25, 1944 was the TA-22, the former Italian destroyer Giuseppi Missori. The date and the place match the group mission report. However, the TA-22 had been converted by the Germans into a torpedo boat, and was no longer a destroyer. Although it was so heavily damaged that it was put out of action permanently, it did not sink. It was decommissioned on November 8, 1944, and scuttled at Trieste on February 5, 1945. It might as well have been sunk on June 25, 1944, because it never fought the Allies again.[16]

Some sources suggest that the Tuskegee Airmen sank the German ship TA-27, which had been the Italian warship Aurige. The TA-27 was actually sunk on June 9, 1944 off the coast of Elba, west of the Italian peninsula, far from the Adriatic Sea, which is east of the Italian peninsula. The Tuskegee Airmen would not have sunk the TA-27, because the date and place do not match the group mission report.[17]

Myth 6

The "Great Train Robbery"

One of the popular stories about the Tuskegee Airmen is sometimes nicknamed the "Great Train Robbery."According to the story, the 332d Fighter Group would not have been able to escort its assigned bombers all the way to Berlin on the March 24, 1945 mission without larger fuel tanks, and members of the 96th Air Service Group, which serviced the airplanes of the 332d Fighter Group at Ramitelli Air Field in Italy, obtained those larger fuel tanks by force from a train the day before the mission. By working all night, the crews had the P-51s equipped with the larger fuel tanks just in time for the escort mission to succeed.[18]

The story is questionable, however, because the 332d Fighter Group was not the only one of the seven fighter escort groups of the Fifteenth Air Force to fly the Berlin mission. In fact, four other fighter escort groups, the 31st, 52nd, 82nd, and 325th Fighter Groups, all flew on the Berlin mission as well as the 332d Fighter Group. These four other groups would have also needed the larger fuel tanks to take them all the way to Berlin, because all of them had aircraft over the target area on March 24, 1945. Of these other fighter groups on the Berlin mission, three flew P-51s like the 332d Fighter Group. It is not likely that these other fighter groups also had to rob a train in order to obtain the larger fuel tanks they needed to go all the way to Berlin.[19]

James Sheppard was a crew chief in the 301st Fighter Squadron, and took part in preparing P-51s of the 332d Fighter Group for the March 24, 1945 mission to Berlin during the night before the mission. As an experienced aircraft maintenance technician, he did not experience any difficulty in mounting larger fuel tanks to the wings of the P-51s he was maintaining so that they could carry out the mission to Berlin. He did not remember the maintenance personnel needing to rob any train or warehouse in order to obtain the larger fuel tanks they needed for the mission.[20]

The legend might have been based on the fact that the larger 110-gallon auxiliary fuel tanks were delivered to Ramitelli by truck, not from the depot at Foggia, where the smaller fuel tanks had been obtained, but from a railhead at Chieuti instead. On March 23, 1945, the 55th Air Service Squadron of the 380th Air Service Group dispatched trucks from the depot at Foggia to the railhead at Chieuti for fuel tanks. The squadron's diary entry for 24 March notes that it received "one trailer load of 110 gal auxiliary tanks for 366th Air Service Squadron." The 366th Air Service Squadron was based at Ramitelli, Italy, with the 332d Fighter Group, to service its P-51 aircraft. Another 55th Air Service Squadron diary entry in March 1945 notes that the squadron also used trucks to deliver 110-gallon fuel tanks from Chieuti to the 52d Fighter Group, which, like the 332d Fighter Group, flew P-51s for the Fifteenth Air Force and which was based near Ramitelli.[21] The fact that trucks delivered the larger fuel tanks not from the depot at Foggia, as the smaller fuel tanks had been, but from the railhead at Chieuti instead, might have evolved into a "we had to rob a train" story.

The larger 110-gallon fuel tanks the 332nd Fighter Group needed for the Berlin mission were not new to the 332nd Fighter Group. The group had used those larger tanks in previous months. Indications are that the supply ran out just before the Berlin mission. The group did need to obtain the larger tanks again for the longer mission, but the group did not have to suddenly find out how to adapt the tanks to fit their P-51s, since it had used such larger tanks on previous missions.[22]

Myth 7

Superiority

Another popular story, not verified by any historical evidence, is that the members of the 332d Fighter Group were so much better at bomber escort than the members of the other six fighter groups in the Fifteenth Air Force, the bombardment groups requested that they be escorted by the 332d Fighter Group. According to the story, white fighter pilots, unlike the black ones, abandoned the bombers they were assigned to escort in order to chase after enemy fighters to increase their aerial victory credit scores for fame and glory. One version of this story appears in Kai Wright's book *Soldiers of Freedom: An Illustrated History of African Americans in the Armed Forces* (New York: Black Dog and Leventhal Publishers, 2002), p. 181: "Throughout the war, it [the 332d Fighter Group] flew bomber escorts- duty rejected by white pilots because it didn't offer as much opportunity to earn kills, and thus praise and promotion- and earned a reputation as the air force's most reliable escort."[23]

There were a great many fighter escort groups in the Army Air Forces during World War II. In Europe they served with the Eighth and Fifteenth Air Forces. The Fifteenth Air Force alone had seven such fighter groups. To say that the 332d Fighter Group did a better job at escorting bombers than any of the other fighter groups is very difficult to prove from an examination of the World War II documents.

The World War II records of the Fifteenth Air Force's seven fighter groups and twenty-one bombardment groups, and the daily mission reports of the Fifteenth Air Force between June 1944 and April 1945, do not support the claim that the 332d Fighter Group was the only one to provide effective fighter escort protection. The evidence shows that all of the fighter groups, black or white, were flying the same kinds of escort missions. Each day, each group was assigned by Fifteenth Air Force headquarters to escort a bombardment wing or set of bombardment wings at certain times and places, and apparently each flew, for the most part, as assigned.[24] None of the twenty-one bomber groups was stationed at the same airfield as any of the seven fighter groups.[25] The assignments rotated, and one fighter group was not always assigned to escort the same bombardment wing or wings, or to provide the same kind of escort day after day. For example, sometimes a group would be assigned penetration escort, sometimes withdrawal escort, sometimes escort over the target, and sometimes a combination of them. The daily mission reports show that all the groups were flying the same kinds of missions, for the most part, and do not indicate that only one was escorting in an effective way. On many days, more than one fighter group was escorting many bomber groups. Because the assignments were made on a rotational basis by headquarters, apparently without discrimination, the idea that bombardment crews could request one fighter group over another for escort duty, and get it, is not likely.

The history of the Fifteenth Air Force covering November 1943-May 1945, vol. I, notes that "Before the summer of 1944, the fighters always maintained close escort. The original policy of the Air Force, in fact, stipulated that the fighters were never to leave the bombers in order to make an attack unless enemy aircraft were obviously preparing to strike at the bomber formation. As enemy fighter opposition declined, however, one squadron, at the discretion of the group commander, was sometimes detached for a fighter sweep against the enemy. This was done on withdrawal only, and in no case before the bombers had reached the target."[26]

Another interesting quote from the same document: "During the counter-air campaign early in 1944, a particularly high level of efficiency was reached by the escort fighters. On four consecutive days in February, heavy bomber penetrations into Germany were covered by an escort of P-38s and P-47s. Bomber pilots reported that the cover provided on these missions was the best ever furnished in the Air Force up to that time." It bears noting that the 332d Fighter Group had not started to escort Fifteenth Air Force bombers yet. The 332d Fighter Group started escorting bombers for the Fifteenth Air Force in June 1944. From this important document, it seems clear that the policy of the Fifteenth Air Force in the Mediterranean Theater of Operations, unlike the policy of the Eighth Air Force after Lt. Gen. James Doolittle took charge of it, was to furnish close escort for the bombers, and not leave them to go after enemy fighters in the distance. Apparently the 332d Fighter Group was not the only fighter group providing close escort in the Fifteenth Air Force, and doing it well enough for the bomber crews to express appreciation, although they did not specify any particular fighter group.[27]

All of the bombardment groups were stationed at bases miles away from the 332d Fighter Group at Ramitelli Air Field in Italy, and their personnel had little or no interaction with the personnel of the fighter groups that escorted them. Most of them did not have the option of choosing one group over another.

Table VI: Stations of Fifteenth Air Force Groups, June 1944–May 1945

Group	Wing	Airfield	Predominate aircraft type
2 Bombardment	5 Bombardment	Amendola, Italy	B-17
97 Bombardment	5 Bombardment	Amendola, Italy	B-17
99 Bombardment	5 Bombardment	Tortorella, Italy	B-17
301 Bombardment	5 Bombardment	Lucera, Italy	B-17
463 Bombardment	5 Bombardment	Celone, Italy	B-17
483 Bombardment	5 Bombardment	Sterparone, Italy	B-17
98 Bombardment	47 Bombardment	Lecce, Italy	B-24
376 Bombardment	47 Bombardment	San Pancrazio, Italy	B-24
449 Bombardment	47 Bombardment	Grottaglie, Italy	B-24
450 Bombardment	47 Bombardment	Manduria, Italy	B-24
451 Bombardment	49 Bombardment	Castelluccio, Italy	B-24
461 Bombardment	49 Bombardment	Torretto, Italy	B-24
484 Bombardment	49 Bombardment	Torretto, Italy	B-24
460 Bombardment	55 Bombardment	Spinazzola, Italy	B-24
464 Bombardment	55 Bombardment	Pantanella, Italy	B-24

465 Bombardment	55 Bombardment	Partanella, Italy	B-24
485 Bombardment	55 Bombardment	Venosa, Italy	B-24
454 Bombardment	304 Bombardment	San Giovanni, Italy	B-24
455 Bombardment	304 Bombardment	San Giovanni, Italy	B-24
456 Bombardment	304 Bombardment	Stornara, Italy	B-24
459 Bombardment	304 Bombardment	Giulia, Italy	B-24
1 Fighter	305 Fighter	Salsola, then Vincenzo, then Salsolo, then Lesina, Italy	P-38
14 Fighter	305 Fighter	Triolo, Italy	P-38
82 Fighter	305 Fighter	Vincenzo, Italy	P-38
31 Fighter	306 Fighter	San Severo, then Mondolfo, Italy	P-51
52 Fighter	306 Fighter	Madna, then Piagiolino, Italy	P-51
325 Fighter	306 Fighter	Lesina, then Rimini, then Mondolfo, Italy	P-51
332 Fighter	306 Fighter	Ramitelli, Italy	P-51

Source: Maurer Maurer, *Air Force Combat Units of World War II* (Washington, DC: Office of Air Force History, 1983).

At least one of the bombardment groups had become acquainted with the 332d Fighter Group, and knew it consisted of black pilots flying bomber escort duty. On December 29, 1944, eighteen B-24 bombers were forced by bad weather to land at Ramitelli Air Field in Italy, the home base of the 332d Fighter Group, which was flying P-51s. Seventeen of those bombers came from the 485th Bombardment Group, and the other one came from the 455th Bombardment Group. Most of the white bomber crews spent five days with the Tuskegee Airmen, enjoying their hospitality at a very crowded base. The 332d Fighter Group left a note in each bomber noting that the 332d Fighter Group's red-tailed escort fighters were there to protect them on their bombing missions. If any bomber crews requested that the 332d Fighter Group escort them, they probably belonged to the 485th or 455th Bombardment Groups, some of whose personnel had met members of the 332d Fighter Group and shared accommodations with them. The request would have been based on the bomber crews' experience at Ramitelli, and not because the 332d Fighter Group had demonstrated its obvious superiority to the other fighter groups of the Fifteenth Air Force.[28]

That might be one reason Col. Benjamin O. Davis, Jr. flew a P-51 aircraft with "By Request" painted on the side.[29] There is another explanation. During the spring of 1944, Major General Ira C. Eaker, commander of the Mediterranean Allied Air Forces, reassigned the 332d Fighter Group from the Twelfth Air Force to the Fifteenth Air Force because he sought its help with bomber escort duty.[30] In effect, Eaker had "requested" the 332d Fighter Group for the bomber escort mission, even before the group had flown any heavy bomber escort missions.

At times, the bombardment crews would mistake one set of escorts for another. For example, World War II B-24 bomber pilot John Sonneborn remembered gratefully that his aircraft was saved by a red-tailed P-51 pilot when he was flying a mission to Ploesti, Rumania, on May 5, 1944. He assumed that he had been escorted by a Tuskegee Airman, since he learned after the war that they had flown red-tailed P-51s in his theater. What Mr. Sonneborn did not realize was that the 332d Fighter Group did not begin flying missions to escort heavy bombers such as

B-24s until June 1944, and the 332d Fighter Group did not begin flying P-51 aircraft until July 1944. If Sonneborn were saved by a pilot in a red-tailed P-51, that fighter pilot must have belonged to the 31st Fighter Group, because the 31st Fighter Group escorted B-24s to Ploesti on May 5, 1944, and the tails of the 31st Fighter Group P-51s were painted with red stripes. After the war, bomber crews sometimes gave fighter escort credit to the wrong group.[31]

In November 1945, the War Department published a report called "Policy for Utilization of Negro Manpower in the Post-War Army." Since the report had been prepared by a committee of generals headed by Lt. Gen. Alvan C. Gillem, Jr., it was sometimes called the "Gillem Report." Part of the report compared the four P-51 fighter escort groups of the Fifteenth Air Force, which included the all-black 332nd Fighter Group and the all-white 31st, 52nd, 325th, and 332nd Fighter Groups (the other three fighter escort groups of the Fifteenth Air Force, the 1st, 14th, and 82nd, flew P-38 aircraft). While the report praised the 332d Fighter Group for successfully escorting bombers, it also criticized the group for having fewer aerial victory credits than the other groups because it did not aggressively chase enemy fighters to shoot them down, but stayed with the bombers it was escorting. The report also claimed that each of the three white P-51 fighter groups shot down more than twice as many aircraft as it lost in combat, but that the 332d Fighter Group lost more of its own aircraft in combat than it destroyed of the enemy. The implication is that the black 332d Fighter Group might have lost fewer bombers it escorted than the other three white P-51 fighter escort groups, it also shot down the least number of enemy aircraft. Depending on what the criterion was, the 332d Fighter Group was the worst and also the best at the same time.[32]

Table VII: Comparison of Fifteenth Air Force P-51 Fighter Groups

Fighter Group	Predominant race	Victories per aircraft lost in combat
31st	White	2.49
52nd	White	2.08
325th	White	2.22
332nd	Black	0.66

Source: "Policy for Utilization of Negro Manpower in the Post-War Army," Report of War Department Special Board on Negro Manpower, November 1945, Air Force Historical Research Agency call number 170.2111-1, November 1945), section on historical evaluation of the Negro's Military Service, subsection 9, evaluation of combat performance of the Negro in World War II, under g., "combat aviation," p. 15.

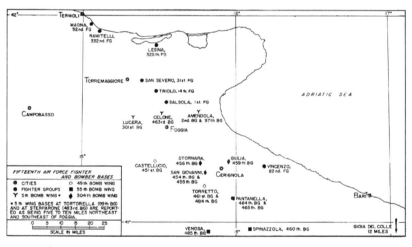

Fifteenth Air Force airfields in eastern Italy during late 1944.

Myth 8

The Tuskegee Airmen Units
were All Black

Unfortunately, many articles and references to the Tuskegee Airmen are so short that they mislead the reader into thinking that all the members of the Tuskegee Airmen organizations were black, and that they faced unanimous opposition from white members of the Army Air Forces with whom they had to struggle for equal opportunity even as they struggled against the overseas Axis enemy. In truth, white officers were always involved in the Tuskegee Airmen experience, sometimes hindering their progress, but more often facilitating it.

The most famous of the Tuskegee Airmen military organizations were the 99th Fighter Squadron, the first black flying unit in the American military; the 332d Fighter Group, the first black fighter group; and the 477th Bombardment Group, the first black bomber group. All of these Tuskegee Airmen military organizations began with both black and white members. The first three commanders of the 99th Fighter Squadron (originally called the 99th Pursuit Squadron) were white. They included Captain Harold R. Maddux, 2nd Lt. Clyde H. Bynum, and Captain Alonzo S. Ward. The first two commanders of the 332d Fighter Group were white. They included Lt. Col. Sam W. Westbrook and Col. Robert R. Selway. The first commander of the 477th Bombardment Group, after it was activated as a predominantly black group, was white. He was Col. Robert R. Selway (who had earlier commanded the 332nd Fighter Group). All of these military organizations eventually became all-black, but they did not begin that way. Of course, the white members of the organizations were in leadership positions, and black officers did not command white officers.[33]

Many of the flight instructors at Tuskegee were white. This was true at all three of the bases around Tuskegee, including Kennedy Field, where civilian pilot training took place; at Moton Field, where the primary flight training occurred; and at Tuskegee Army Air Field, where the basic, advanced, and transition training was completed. White officers retained leadership positions in the flying training organizations at Moton Field and Tuskegee Army Air Field throughout World War II.[34]

For more than a year before the 99th Fighter Squadron was assigned to the 332d Fighter Group, it served in combat overseas while attached to various white fighter groups, as if it were one of the squadrons of those groups. In effect, those groups included both black and white personnel while the 99th Fighter Squadron was attached to them. Some of the members of the 99th Fighter Squadron, which by then had become an all-black organization, resented being assigned to the 332d Fighter Group, because they had become accustomed to serving in white groups, flying alongside white fighter squadrons, and did not relish being placed with the black fighter group simply because they were also black. In a sense, it was a step back toward more segregation. At any rate, many Tuskegee Airmen during World War II served in units with both black and white personnel, although as the war progressed, their organizations increasingly became all-black.[35]

To be sure, some of the white officers who were in command of Tuskegee Airmen opposed equal opportunities for them. Colonel William Momyer of the 33rd Fighter Group opposed the continued combat role of the 99th Fighter Squadron when it was attached to his group, and Colonel Robert Selway, commander of the 477th Bombardment Group at Freeman Field, attempted to enforce segregated officers' clubs at that base, and had many of the Tuskegee Airmen arrested for opposing his policy.[36] But for every white officer who discouraged equal opportunity for the Tuskegee Airmen under their command, there were other white officers who sincerely worked for their success. They included Forrest Shelton, who instructed pilots in civilian and primary pilot training at Kennedy and Moton Fields near Tuskegee; Major William T. Smith, who supervised primary pilot training at Moton Field; Captain Robert

M. Long, a flight instructor who taught the first Tuskegee Airmen pilots to graduate from advanced pilot training at Tuskegee Army Air Field; Colonel Noel Parrish, commander of the pilot training at Tuskegee Army Air Field; and Colonel Earl E. Bates, commander of the 79th Fighter Group for most of the time the 99th Fighter Squadron was attached to it (from October 1943 to April 1944.)[37]

Colonel Noel Parrish, commander of Tuskegee Army Air Field, where black cadets received their basic and advanced flying training during World War II.

Myth 9

All Tuskegee Airmen were Fighter Pilots who Flew Red-Tailed P-51s to Escort Bombers

Museum displays, World War II history books, magazine articles, pamphlets, newspaper articles, television programs, and even movies sometimes describe only one part of the Tuskegee Airmen story, misleading readers or observers into thinking that all the Tuskegee Airmen flew red-tailed P-51s on bomber escort missions deep into enemy territory. The Tuskegee Airmen story is much more complex than that. In fact, the Tuskegee Airmen flew four kinds of fighter aircraft in combat, and also bombers not in combat. Many of the Tuskegee Airmen who flew in combat during World War II and earned distinguished records never saw a red-tailed P-51. A good example is Charles Dryden, who returned from Italy months before any of the Tuskegee Airmen flew any P-51s overseas, and months before they received the assignment to escort heavy bombers deep into enemy territory.[38]

To be sure, the most famous Tuskegee Airmen flew red-tailed P-51 Mustangs to escort Fifteenth Air Force heavy bombers on raids deep into enemy territory, but not all of them did so. Before July 1944, the 99th Fighter Squadron flew P-40 fighters on patrol and air-to-ground attack missions against enemy targets on tactical missions for the Twelfth Air Force. Sometimes these missions involved escorting medium bombers, but more often they involved supporting Allied surface forces and defending them from attack by enemy aircraft in Italy. During June 1944, the 332d

Fighter Group flew P-47 aircraft on bomber escort missions. Before then, the group and its three fighter squadrons flew P-39 aircraft on tactical missions for the Twelfth Air Force, supporting Allied ground forces in Italy. Neither the P-39s nor the P-40s had red tails. Only in July 1944 was the 99th Fighter Squadron assigned to the 332d Fighter Group, and only in that month did the group begin to fly red-tailed P-51s. The group painted the tails of the aircraft red because the Fifteenth Air Force had seven fighter escort groups, including three P-38 and four P-51 groups. All four of the P-51 groups had distinctively-painted tails. The 31st Fighter Group had red-striped tails; the 52nd Fighter Group had yellow tails; the 325th Fighter Group had black and yellow checkerboard-patterned tails. The tails of the 332d Fighter Group were painted solid red.[39] The assigned colors for each group helped distinguish it from other groups in large formations flying to, from, and over enemy targets. The various colored tails also helped bomber crews tell which groups were escorting them, and whether distant fighters were friend or foe.

Some of the African-American pilots who trained at Tuskegee Army Air Field during World War II never became fighter pilots at all. They became bomber pilots, and were assigned after their Tuskegee training to the 477th Bombardment Group, which flew twin-engined B-25s. That group never deployed overseas to take part in combat during the war.[40]

Myth 10

Eleanor Roosevelt Persuaded the President to Establish a Black Flying Unit in the Army Air Corps

Contrary to a persistent myth, Eleanor Roosevelt's visit to Tuskegee Institute at the end of March 1941, during which she was given an airplane ride by Charles Anderson, who taught civilian pilot training at the institute, did not result in her convincing her husband, President Franklin D. Roosevelt, to establish a black flying unit in the Army Air Corps.[41]

In fact, the decision to establish a black flying unit in the Army Air Corps had been announced by the War Department on January 16, 1941, more than two months before Eleanor Roosevelt's visit to Tuskegee. The announcement included mention of plans to train support personnel for the unit at Chanute Field, Illinois, followed by pilot training at Tuskegee. On March 19, 1941, the War Department constituted the first black flying unit, the 99th Pursuit Squadron, and on March 22, the unit was activated at Chanute Field.[42] According to the plans, it would move to Tuskegee later, when facilities for the training of the pilots had been constructed.

Eleanor Roosevelt undoubtedly supported the efforts to establish black flying training at Tuskegee, and her visit to Tuskegee Institute at the end of March 1941 encouraged contributions for the building of a primary flying base at Tuskegee (which later became Moton Field), but she did not convince her husband the President to establish the first black flying unit, because the unit had already been planned, constituted, and activated by the time of her Tuskegee visit.

Aerial photograph of Tuskegee Army Air Field during World War II.

Myth 11

The Tuskegee Airmen Earned 150 Distinguished Flying Crosses during World War II

For many years the Tuskegee Airmen were said to have earned 150 Distinguished Flying Crosses during World War II. According to Dr. Roscoe Brown, an original Tuskegee Airmen who earned his own Distinguished Flying Cross (DFC), 150 is the usual number one hears or reads for DFCs that were earned by Tuskegee Airmen. He said the number was based on the book, *The Tuskegee Airmen: The Men Who Changed a Nation*, by Charles Francis. Francis noted that there was evidence for 95 DFCs awarded to Tuskegee Airmen, but possibly there were as many as 150.[43]

Craig Huntly of the Tuskegee Airmen Incorporated's Harry A. Sheppard historical research committee checked all the Fifteenth Air Force general orders that awarded DFCs to Tuskegee Airmen, and found 95 had been awarded. He knew that the Tuskegee Airmen units in combat had also served with the Twelfth Air Force, before joining the Fifteenth Air Force, and that Twelfth Air Force general orders would also probably note additional DFCs awarded to Tuskegee Airmen. However, Huntly found only one Twelfth Air Force general order that awarded a DFC to a Tuskegee Airman. It recognized the aerial victory credit of Charles B. Hall, the first black pilot in military service to shoot down an enemy airplane. He found no other Twelfth Air Force orders that awarded DFCs to Tuskegee Airmen. Tuskegee Airmen who earned other aerial victory credits, while flying with the Twelfth Air Force, earned Air Medals instead of DFCs. The total number of DFCs awarded to Tuskegee Airmen was therefore was 96: 95 of which were awarded by Fifteenth Air Force orders, and 1 awarded by a Twelfth Air Force order. Moreover, one Tuskegee Airman, Captain William A. Campbell, earned two DFCs. Therefore, 95 Tuskegee Airmen earned DFCs, but 96 DFCs were awarded to Tuskegee Airmen.

I searched through every one of the orders that Huntly listed, and found the dates of the events for which each of the Tuskegee Airmen DFCs were awarded. I placed the events in chronological order so that I could include them in my larger Tuskegee Airmen Chronology. The correct number of DFCs earned by the Tuskegee Airmen, for which there is documentation, is 96, not 150. The table below shows the numbers of all the Fifteenth and Twelfth Air Force general orders that awarded DFCs to Tuskegee Airmen.

Table VIII: Chronological List of Tuskegee Airmen Distinguished Flying Cross Winners, by date of the Action for which each DFC was Awarded

Date	Name	Fighter Squadron of 332D Fighter Group	General Order Number and Date of Issue (all issued by Fifteenth Air Force except first one)
28 Jan 1944	Capt. Charles B. Hall	99	64, 22 May 1944 (12 AF)
12 May 1944	Capt. Howard L. Baugh	99	4041, 19 Oct 1944
21 May 1944	1 Lt. Charles W. Tate	99	449, 31 Jan 1945
27 May 1944	1 Lt. Clarence W. Dart	99	449, 31 Jan 1945
4 June 1944	Capt. Edward L. Toppins	99	4041, 19 Oct 1944
4 June 1944	Capt. Leonard M. Jackson	99	4876, 5 Dec 1944
5 June 1944	Capt. Elwood T. Driver	99	449, 31 Jan 1945
9 June 1944	Col. Benjamin O. Davis, Jr.	(332 Fighter Gp)	2972, 31 Aug 1944
12 July 1944	Capt. Joseph D. Elsberry	301	2466, 10 Aug 1944
16 July 1944	Capt. Alphonza W. Davis	(332 Fighter Gp)	3541, 22 Sep 1944
16 July 1944	1 Lt. William W. Green	302	49, 3 Jan 1945
17 July 1944	1 Lt. Luther H. Smith	302	5068, 18 Dec 1944
17 July 1944	1 Lt. Laurence D. Wilkins	302	49, 3 Jan 1945
18 July 1944	2 Lt. Clarence D. Lester	100	3167, 6 Sep 1944

18 July 1944	1 Lt. Jack D. Holsclaw	100	3167, 6 Sep 1944
18 July 1944	Capt. Andrew D. Turner	100	4009, 17 Oct 1944
18 July 1944	1 Lt. Walter J. A. Palmer	100	654, 13 Feb 1945
18 July 1944	1 Lt. Charles P. Bailey	99	3484, 29 May 1945
20 July 1944	Capt. Henry B. Perry	99	4993, 14 Dec 1944
25 July 1944	Capt. Harold E. Sawyer	301	4876, 5 Dec 1944
27 July 1944	1 Lt. Edward C. Gleed	(332 Fighter Gp)	3106, 4 Sep 1944
12 August 1944	Capt. Lee Rayford	301	5068, 18 Dec 1944
12 August 1944	Capt. Woodrow W. Crockett	100	49, 3 Jan 1945
12 August 1944	Capt. William T. Mattison	100	49, 3 Jan 1945
12 August 1944	1 Lt. Freddie E. Hutchins	302	49, 3 Jan 1945
12 August 1944	1 Lt. Lawrence B. Jefferson	301	49, 3 Jan 1945
12 August 1944	1 Lt. Lowell C. Steward	100	231, 15 Jan 1945
14 August 1944	Capt. Melvin T. Jackson	302	3689, 29 Sep 1944
14 August 1944	1 Lt. Gwynne W. Pierson	302	287, 19 Jan 1945
14 August 1944	Capt. Arnold W. Cisco	301	839, 21 Feb 1945
14 August 1944	Capt. Alton F. Ballard	301	1153, 5 Mar 1945
24 August 1944	1 Lt. John F. Briggs	100	49, 3 Jan 1945
24 August 1944	1 Lt. William H. Thomas	302	449, 31 Jan 1945

Date	Name	Group	Citation
27 August 1944	Capt. Wendell O. Pruitt	302	3950, 15 Oct 1944
27 August 1944	Capt. Dudley M. Watson	302	4009, 17 Oct 1944
27 August 1944	1 Lt. Roger Romine	302	5068, 18 Dec 1944
30 August 1944	Capt. Clarence H. Bradford	301	1811, 27 Mar 1945
8 September 1944	Maj. George S. Roberts	(332 Fighter Gp)	137, 8 Jan 1945
8 September 1944	1 Lt. Heber C. Houston	99	3484, 29 May 1945
4 October 1944	1 Lt. Samuel L. Curtis	100	158, 10 Jan 1945
4 October 1944	1 Lt. Dempsey Morgan	100	231, 15 Jan 1945
4 October 1944	Capt. Claude B. Govan	301	255, 16 Jan 1945
4 October 1944	1 Lt. Herman A. Lawson	99	449, 31 Jan 1945
4 October 1944	1 Lt. Willard L. Woods	100	449, 31 Jan 1945
6 October 1944	1 Lt. Alva N. Temple	99	231, 15 Jan 1945
6 October 1944	Capt. Lawrence E. Dickson	100	287, 19 Jan 1945
6 October 1944	1 Lt Edward M. Thomas	99	517, 6 Feb 1945
6 October 1944	1 Lt. Robert L. Martin	100	839, 21 Feb 1945
6 October 1944	Capt. Robert J. Friend	301	1811, 27 Mar 1945
11 October 1944	Capt. William A. Campbell	99	4215, 28 Oct 1944
11 October 1944	1 Lt. George E. Gray	99	4425, 10 Nov 1944
11 October 1944	1 Lt. Felix J. Kirkpatrick	302	4876, 5 Dec 1944

11 October 1944	1 Lt. Richard S. Harder	99	836, 21 Feb 1945
12 October 1944	1 Lt. Lee Archer	302	4876, 5 Dec 1944
12 October 1944	Capt. Milton R. Brooks	302	255, 16 Jan 1945
12 October 1944	1 Lt. Frank E. Roberts	100	287, 19 Jan 1945
12 October 1944	1 Lt. Spurgeon N. Ellington	100	449, 31 Jan 1945
12 October 1944	1 Lt. Leonard F. Turner	301	836, 21 Feb 1945
12 October 1944	Capt. Armour G. McDaniel	301	1430, 15 Mar 1945
12 October 1944	Capt. Stanley L. Harris	301	1811, 27 Mar 1945
12 October 1944	1 Lt. Marion R. Rodgers	301	1811, 27 Mar 1945
12 October 1944	1 Lt. Quitman C. Walker	99	3484, 29 May 1945
13 October 1944	1 Lt. Milton S. Hays	99	719, 16 Feb 1945
14 October 1944	1 Lt. George M. Rhodes, Jr.	100	49, 3 Jan 1945
21 October 1944	Capt. Vernon V. Haywood	302	5068, 18 Dec 1944
16 November 1944	Capt. Luke J. Weathers	302	5228, 28 Dec 1944
19 November 1944	Capt. Albert H. Manning	99	4876, 5 Dec 1944
19 November 1944	Capt. John Daniels	99	5068, 18 Dec 1944
19 November 1944	1 Lt. William N. Alsbrook	99	836, 21 Feb 1945
19 November 1944	1 Lt. Norman W. Scales	100	836, 21 Feb 1945
16 February 1945	Capt. Emile G. Clifton	99	3484, 29 May 1945

Date	Name		Order
17 February 1945	Capt. Louis G. Purnell	301	2362, 14 Apr 1945
25 February 1945	1 Lt. Roscoe C. Brown	100	1430, 15 Mar 1945
25 February 1945	1 Lt. Reid E. Thompson	100	2270, 11 Apr 1945
12 March 1945	Capt. Walter M. Downs	301	3484, 29 May 1945
14 March 1945	1 Lt. Shelby F. Westbrook	99	2362, 14 Apr 1945
14 March 1945	1 Lt. Hannibal M. Cox	99	3031, 5 May 1945
14 March 1945	2 Lt. Vincent I. Mitchell	99	3031, 5 May 1945
14 March 1945	1 Lt. Thomas P. Braswell	99	3484, 29 May 1945
14 March 1945	2 Lt. John W. Davis	99	3484, 29 May 1945
16 March 1945	1 Lt Roland W. Moody	301	2834, 28 Apr 1945
16 March 1945	1 Lt. Henry R. Peoples	301	2834, 28 Apr 1945
16 March 1945	1 Lt. William S. Price III	301	2834, 28 Apr 1945
24 March 1945	1 Lt. Earl R. Lane	100	2834, 28 Apr 1945
24 March 1945	2 Lt. Charles V. Brantley	100	2834, 28 Apr 1945
31 March 1945	1 Lt. Robert W. Williams	100	3484, 29 May 1945
31 March 1945	1 Lt. Bertram W. Wilson Jr.	100	3484, 29 May 1945
1 April 1945	1 Lt. Charles L. White	301	2834, 28 Apr 1945
1 April 1945	1 Lt. John E. Edwards	301	3484, 29 May 1945
1 April 1945	1 Lt. Harry T. Stewart Jr.	301	3484, 29 May 1945

1 April 1945	2 Lt. Carl E. Carey	301	3484, 29 May 1945
15 April 1945	Capt. Gordon M. Rapier	301	3324, 21 May 1945
15 April 1945	1 Lt. Gentry E. Barnes	99	3484, 29 May 1945
15 April 1945	Capt. William A. Campbell	99	3484, 29 May 1945
15 April 1945	1 Lt. Jimmy Lanham	301	3484, 29 May 1945
26 April 1945	1 Lt. Thomas W. Jefferson	301	3343, 22 May 1945

Conclusion

Whoever dispenses with the myths that have come to circulate around the Tuskegee Airmen in the many decades since World War II emerges with a greater appreciation for what they actually accomplished. If they did not demonstrate that they were far superior to the members of the six non-black fighter escort groups of the Fifteenth Air Force with which they served, they certainly demonstrated that they were not inferior to them, either. Moreover, they began at a line farther back, overcoming many more obstacles on the way to combat. The Tuskegee Airmen proved that they were equal to the other fighter pilots with whom they served heroically during World War II. Their exemplary performance opened the door for the racial integration of the military services, beginning with the Air Force, and contributed ultimately to the end of racial segregation in the United States.

DANIEL L. HAULMAN, PhD
Chief, Organizational Histories Branch
Air Force Historical Research Agency

Notes

1 Alan L. Gropman, *The Air Force Integrates, 1945–1964* (Washington, DC: Office of Air Force History, 1985), p. 2–3.

2 Alan L. Gropman, *The Air Force Integrates, 1945–1964* (Washington, DC: Office of Air Force History, 1985), p. 12; *Ulysses Lee, The Employment of Negro Troops* (Washington, DC: Office of the Chief of Military History, United States Army, 1966), 157.

3 Air Force Historical Research Agency call number 134.65-496.

4 Daniel L. Haulman, "Tuskegee Airmen-Escorted Bombers Lost to Enemy Aircraft," paper prepared at the Air Force Historical Research Agency. This paper is based on histories of the 332d Fighter Group, daily mission reports of the Fifteenth Air Force, and Missing Air Crew Reports that show the times, locations, and causes of aircraft losses.

5 Interview of General Benjamin O. Davis, Jr., by Alan Gropman, AFHRA call number K239.0512-122.

6 Fifteenth Air Force General Order 2972 issued on Aug. 31, 1944.

7 332d Fighter Group histories, under call number GP-332-HI at the Air Force Historical Research Agency; Fifteenth Air Force daily mission folders, under call number 670.332 at the Air Force Historical Research Agency, Missing Air Crew Reports, indexed and filed on microfiche in the Archives Branch of the Air Force Historical Research Agency.

8 Oliver North, *War Stories III* (Washington, DC: Regnery Publishing, Inc., 2005), p. 152.

9 Monthly histories of the 332d Fighter Group, June 1944-April 1945; Fifteenth Air Force General Order 2350 dated Aug. 6, 1944; Fifteenth Air Force General Order 4287 dated Nov. 1, 1944.

10 Charles E. Francis, *The Tuskegee Airmen* (Boston: Bruce Humpries, Inc., 1955), pp. 92 and 194.

11 The author heard this statement repeated at one of the four Tuskegee Airmen Incorporated national conventions he attended in the successive years 2007, 2008, 2009, and 2010. Dr. Roscoe Brown did not make the claim himself, but he was aware of it. The claim also was published in George Norfleet's book, *A Pilot's Journey: Memoirs of a Tuskegee Airman, Curtis Christopher Robinson* (Washington, DC: Robnor Publishing, 2006 and 2008), p. 217.

12 Fifteenth Air Force General Order 2293 dated Apr. 12, 1945.

13 USAAF (European Theater) Credits for the Destruction of Enemy Aircraft in Air-to-Air Combat, World War 2, Victory List No. 5, Frank J. Olynyk, May 1987; USAAF (Mediterranean Theater) Credits for the Destruction of Enemy Aircraft in Air-to-Air Combat, World War 2, Victory List No. 6, Frank J. Olynyk, June 1987; USAF Historical Study No. 85, USAF Credits for the Destruction of Enemy Aircraft, World War II, Albert F. Simpson Historical Research Center, 1978; *Combat Squadrons of the Air Force, World War II*, edited by Maurer Maurer, 1969; *Air Force Combat Units of World War II*, edited by Maurer Maurer, 1983. This information was compiled by Ms. Patsy Robertson, a historian at the Air Force Historical Research Agency.

14 John B. Holway, *Red Tails, Black Wings* (Las Cruces, NM: Yucca Tree Press, 1997), p. 262.

15 Fifteenth Air Force General Orders 2525, dated Apr. 19, 1945 and 2709 dated Apr. 24, 1945.

16 332d Fighter Group history for June 1944; 332d Fighter Group mission report for June 25, 1944; David Brown, *Warship Losses of World War II* (Annapolis, MD: Naval Institute Press, 1990); "Fighting Ships of the World," website of Ivan Gogin (http://www.navypedia.org/ships/germany/ger_tb_ta22.htm).

17 Myth contained in Wikipedia under Ariete Class Torpedo Boat; more correct information from H. P. Willmott's *The Last Century of Sea Power, volume 2, From Washington to Tokyo, 1922–1945* (Bloomington, Indiana: Indiana University Press, 2010), p. 207.

18 J. Todd Moye, *Freedom Flyers: The Tuskegee Airmen of World War II* (Oxford University Press, 2010), p. 121; *John B. Holway, Red Tails, Black Wings* (Las Cruces, NM: Yucca Tree Press, 1997), p. 260.

19 Narrative Mission Reports of the 31st, 52nd, 82nd, 325th, and 332nd Fighter Groups, contained in the Fifteenth Air Force mission folder for March 24, 1945, AFHRA call number 670.332, March 24, 1945.

20 E-mail from James Sheppard, an original Tuskegee Airmen, and a member of the Tuskegee Airmen Incororated, with whom the author has spoken and corresponded.

21 55th Air Service Squadron history for March 1945. The AFHRA call number is SQ-SV-55-HI Jul 1942-May 1945.

22 55th Air Service Squadron histories for December 1944-March 1945, AFHRA call number SQ-SV-55-HI Jul 1942-May 1945.

23 Kai Wright, *Soldiers of Freedom: An Illustrated History of African Americans in the Armed Forces* (New York: Black Dog and Leventhal Publishers, 2002), p. 181.

24 Fifteenth Air Force daily mission folders, containing narrative mission reports of all the groups flying on missions that day, call number 670.332 at the Air Force Historical Research Agency.

25 Maurer Maurer, *Air Force Combat Units of World War II* (Washington, DC: Office of Air Force History, 1983), under each group designation.

26 History of the Fifteenth Air Force, November 1943-May 1945, vol. I (Air Force Historical Research Agency call number 670.01-1), pp. 277 and 286.

27 History of the Fifteenth Air Force, November 1943-May 1945, vol. I (Air Force Historical Research Agency call number 670.01-1), pp. 286–287.

28 Fifteenth Air Force mission folder for December 29, 1944; 485th Bombardment Group history for January 1945.

29 Benjamin O. Davis, Jr., *Benjamin O. Davis, Jr., American* (Washington, DC: Smithsonian Institution Press, 1991), photograph between pages 54 and 55.

30 332d Fighter Group history, Mar-Apr 1944; 332d Fighter Group War Diary, Apr 1944.

31 Ryan Orr, "Veteran's Life Saved by Tuskegee Airman," *Victorville Daily Press,* November 10, 2008; 332d Fighter Group histories for May, June, and July 1944; 31st Fighter Group history for May 1944; Fifteenth Air Force Daily Mission Folder for May 5, 1955; E. A. *Munday, Fifteenth Air Force Combat Markings, 1943–1945* (London, UK: Beaumont Publications), pp. 15–18.

32 "Policy for Utilization of Negro Manpower in the Post-War Army," Report of War Department Special Board on Negro Manpower, November 1945, Air Force Historical Research Agency call number 170.2111-1, November 1945), section on historical evaluation of the Negro's Military Service, subsection 9, evaluation of combat performance of the Negro in World War II, under g., "combat aviation," p. 15.

33 Lineage and honors histories of the 99th Fighter Squadron, the 332rd Fighter Group, and the 477th Bombardment Group, and their monthly histories from World War II, stored at the Air Force Historical Research Agency.

34 History of Tuskegee Army Flying School and AAF 66th FTD, book published by Wings of America and filed at the Air Force Historical Research Agency under call number 289.28-100.

35 Conversations of the author with various original Tuskegee Airmen that took place during his attendance at five successive Tuskegee Airmen Incorporated national conventions, in 2007, 2008, 2009, 2010, and 2011.

36 Alan L. Gropman, *The Air Force Integrates* (Washington, DC: Office of Air Force History 1985), pp. 12–14 and 17–18.

37 History of Tuskegee Army Flying School and AAF 66th FTD, book published by Wings of America and filed at the Air Force Historical Research Agency under call number 289.28-100; Robert J. Jakeman, *The Divided Skies* (Tuscaloosa: University of Alabama Press, 1992), pp. 264–265; Lineage and honors history of the 53rd Test and Evaluation Group (formerly the 79th Fighter Group) at the Air Force Historical Research Agency.

38 Charles W. Dryden, *A-Train: Memoirs of a Tuskegee Airman* (Tuscaloosa: University of Alabama Press, 1997), pp. 144–147.

39 Lineage and honors histories of the 99th Flying Training Squadron (formerly 99th Fighter Squadron) and 332nd Expeditionary Operations Group (formerly 332nd Fighter Group) at the Air Force Historical Research Agency, in addition to their monthly histories from 1943–1945.

40 477th Fighter Group (formerly 477th Bombardment Group) lineage and honors history, and monthly histories of the 477th Bombardment Group in 1944 and

1945, at the Air Force Historical Research Agency.

41 Conversations of the author with several of the original Tuskegee Airmen at a series of five Tuskegee Airmen Incorporated national conventions between 2007 and 2011.

42 Robert J. Jakeman, *The Divided Skies* (Tuscaloosa, AL: The University of Alabama Press, 1992, p. 221; *Maurer Maurer, Combat Squadrons of the Air Force, World War II* (Washington, DC: United States Government Printing Office, 1969), p. 329.

43 Information from Dr. Roscoe Brown, telephone conversation with Dr. Daniel Haulman on December 13, 2011.

About the Author

Dr. Daniel L. Haulman is Chief, Organizational History Division, at the Air Force Historical Research Agency, where he has worked since 1982. He has authored four books, including *Air Force Aerial Victory Credits: World War I, World War II, Korea, and Vietnam*; *The United States and Air Force and Humanitarian Airlift Operations, 1947–1994*; *One Hundred Years of Flight: USAF Chronology of Significant Air and Space Events, 1903–2002*; and *The Tuskegee Airmen, An Illustrated History: 1939–1949* (NewSouth Books, 2011).

To learn more about Daniel Haulman and *The Tuskegee Airmen, An Illustrated History*, visit www.newsouthbooks.com/tuskegeeairmen.

ALSO BY DANIEL HAULMAN

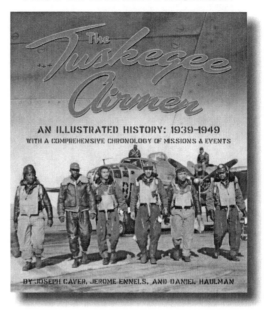

Experience the visual history of the Tuskegee Airmen . . .

Many documentaries, articles, museum exhibits, books, and movies have now treated the subject of the Tuskegee Airmen, the only black American military pilots in World War II. Most of these works have focused on their training and their subsequent accomplishments during combat.

The Tuskegee Airmen: An Illustrated History goes further, using captioned photographs to trace the Airmen through the various stages of training, deployment, and combat in North Africa, Italy, and over occupied Europe. Included for the first time are depictions of the critical support roles of nonflyers: doctors, mechanics, and others, all of whom contributed to the Airmen's success. This volume makes vivid the story of the Tuskegee Airmen and the environments in which they lived, worked, played, fought, and sometimes died.

ISBN 978-1-58838-244-3
Available in hardcover format
Visit www.newsouthbooks.com/tuskegeeairmen

ALSO BY DANIEL HAULMAN

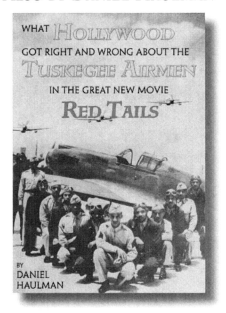

The movie is only the beginning . . .

The new George Lucas movie called *Red Tails* focuses attention on the Tuskegee Airmen of World War II and their combat operations overseas. Loaded with special effects and a great cast, the movie is thrilling and inspiring, but how accurate is it historically? Military historian Daniel Haulman takes an appreciative look at *Red Tails*, comparing it to the actual missions of the Tuskegee Airmen and offering places where interested viewers could study the events further.

"This list of differences between the *Red Tails* depiction of the Tuskegee Airmen and the real Tuskegee Airmen story is not intended to denigrate the movie," Haulman writes in his introduction, "but merely to caution those who might mistakenly take the fictional account as history."

ISBN 978-1-60306-160-5
Available in ebook format
Visit www.newsouthbooks.com/redtails

CPSIA information can be obtained at www.ICGtesting.com
Printed in the USA
LVOW11s1438231015

459498LV00002B/241/P

DEC 08 2015

9 781603 061476